QUIET HERO

HERO

The *Ira Hayes Story*

BY *S. D. NELSON*

LEE & LOW BOOKS INC.   NEW YORK

ACKNOWLEDGMENT
To the courageous people of Alcoholics Anonymous, who offer a cure for the disease of alcoholism that really works. They are individuals who honestly admit that alcohol has them in a stranglehold. Instead of drinking liquor, they regularly attend AA meetings. Like mountain climbers roped together, they journey upward. Cheerfully they welcome anyone who is struggling with alcohol to join them in living a new life of sobriety.

S. D. Nelson

LEE & LOW BOOKS Inc., 95 Madison Avenue, New York, NY 10016
leeandlow.com

Manufactured in China by Jade Productions

Book design by Christy Hale
Book production by The Kids at Our House

The text is set in Amerigo
The illustrations are rendered in acrylic

HC 10 9 8 7 6 5 4 3 2 1
PB 10 9 8 7 6
First Edition

Library of Congress Cataloging-in-Publication Data
Nelson, S. D.
    Quiet hero : the Ira Hayes story / by S. D. Nelson.— 1st ed.
        p. cm.
Summary: "A biography of Native American Ira Hayes, a shy, humble Pima Indian who fought in World War II as a marine and was one of six soldiers to raise the U.S. flag on Iwo Jima, an event immortalized in Joe Rosenthal's famous photograph"—Provided by publisher.
    ISBN 978-1-58430-263-6 (hc)   ISBN 978-1-60060-427-0 (pbk)
1. Hayes, Ira, 1923-1955. 2. Indians of North America—Biography. 3. Marines—United States—Biography. 4. Iwo Jima, Battle of, Japan, 1945. I. Title.
E90.H395N45 2006
940.54'2528—dc22   2005031066

FSC MIX Paper from responsible sources FSC® C001701 www.fsc.org

*Real heroes are not perfect, after all. They are human.
Let us learn from their mistakes as well as their victories.*
— S. D. Nelson

*There is real friendship between us boys. . . . We trust
and depend on one another and that's how it will be
in combat.*
— Ira Hayes

Ira Hayes never wanted to be a hero. Still, he grew up to be just that—a true American hero. He was an ordinary man who did his part to fight for his country in World War II, where an unexpected event won him a place of honor in our hearts.

Ira Hamilton Hayes was born on January 12, 1923, on the Gila River Indian Reservation in Sacaton, Arizona. His people were known as Pima Indians.

Ira was the oldest of four brothers. He was a quiet, shy boy who loved riding a horse bareback and twirling his younger brothers around in an old tire swing.

Ira's family lived in a remote part of the reservation in the Sonoran Desert. The landscape was beautiful, but the land was hot and dry. His parents were poor cotton farmers. The walls of their one-room house were made of dried mud, and the floors were hard-packed dirt. They did not have electric lights or running water. To bathe they used a washcloth, homemade soap, and a washtub full of hot water. The toilet was a hole in the ground in a little shed called an outhouse.

Ira's mother read the Bible aloud and taught him to read. Sometimes at night Ira would read stories to his brothers by the light of a kerosene lantern. At the schools he attended as a young boy, Ira was an average student.

In 1940, when he was a teenager, Ira was sent to Phoenix Indian School, a government-run boarding school for Native Americans.

Life at the boarding school was very different from life on the reservation. The students used running water and toilets that flushed. They followed a strict daily routine. Girls were trained to do housekeeping so they could become maids. Boys were taught manual skills so they could be laborers.

Ira felt out of place. Always quiet, he turned as silent as a stone. He was especially uncomfortable around the girls. Sometimes they teased him and pretended to kiss him. Embarrassed, Ira would run away or quickly climb a tree.

Along with the other boys at school, Ira liked to play sports such as baseball and football. But Ira's shyness kept him in the background. He was never a leader of activities. He was content to be a follower, relatively unnoticed.

Ira grew into a strong young man, but he was deeply lonely. The boarding school did not allow students to go home during the year, so letters were Ira's only way of staying in contact with his family. At night in the crowded dormitory, he often wrote home. He told his family about all he was learning and doing. His parents and brothers were proud of him.

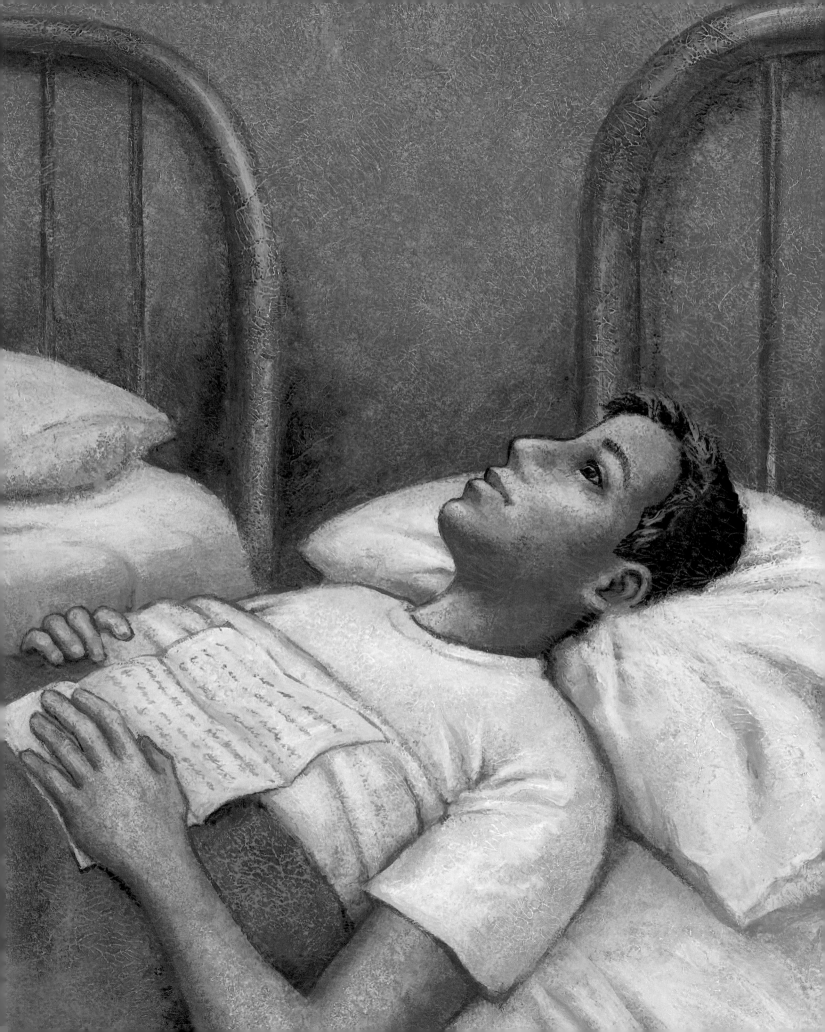

While Ira was away at school, something terrible was happening in the world that would forever change his life. The newspapers and radio carried stories of the Second World War being fought in Europe and Asia. Ira followed these war reports with growing interest.

When the Japanese bombed Pearl Harbor in Hawaii on December 7, 1941, all the young men at Phoenix Indian School wanted to fight back. Ira felt it was his duty as an American to serve his country by becoming a soldier.

In August 1942, at age nineteen, Ira joined the United States Marine Corps. Before he left Ira went home, where everyone gathered to say good-bye. The tribal elders praised his loyalty and patriotism. Ira was ready to carry on the Pima tradition of being an honorable warrior.

Private Ira Hayes was sent to boot camp in San Diego, California, to receive basic training. Many people thought of Indians as fierce fighters, so Ira was allowed to train for combat along with the white soldiers. Other men of color were forced to be cooks or carry supplies.

Ira liked the discipline and challenges of boot camp. The daily routine he was accustomed to at school had prepared him for military regimentation. He and the other new Marines practiced shooting rifles, throwing hand grenades, and other war tactics. After boot camp Ira trained to parachute out of airplanes. Later he was promoted to private first class.

The men in Ira's battalion became best buddies, and Ira finally felt as if he belonged. He was no longer lonely. This was the happiest time in his life.

With their training completed, the Marines boarded transport ships and set out across the Pacific Ocean in March 1943. Over the next two years Ira fought in three major battles against the Japanese in the Pacific. The soldiers endured the hardships of war, and many men, both American and Japanese, were wounded or killed.

Ira did his very best to be an honorable warrior. More than once, in hand-to-hand combat, he proved himself to be just that. His fellow Marines knew they could depend on Ira in a heated fight.

Ira was not shy about being a Marine. In his letters home he said he was proud to be fighting alongside such brave soldiers. He was committed to bringing honor to his family, his people, and his country.

In early 1945 Ira's battalion was sent to Iwo Jima, a tiny, volcanic island south of Japan. With its two airfields, Iwo Jima was an important base for Japan's defense of its homeland. The Japanese were determined to stop the Americans from gaining control of the island. Shells roared overhead and bombs exploded as the Marines landed on the shores of Iwo Jima.

The American soldiers slowly battled their way toward Mount Suribachi at one end of the island. The Japanese had dug caves in the ground and were hiding everywhere. When the shooting became too fierce, Ira and the other soldiers lay face down in the black sand. None of them wanted to die, but the Marines were there to fight, and fight they did.

On February 23, the fifth day of battle, a group of Marines fought its way to the top of Mount Suribachi and planted a small American flag. Even though the battle was still raging, the flag signaled the end of Japanese control of the high ground of Iwo Jima. A little while later a Marine commander decided to put up a bigger flag—one that would be seen for miles. Ira and a small band of soldiers were sent to do this.

Upon the battle-torn summit of Mount Suribachi, Ira and another Marine looked for a flagpole. They found a long iron pipe amid the rubble. A third Marine attached the bigger flag to the pipe. Then three more men joined the effort to raise the heavy flagpole.

Joe Rosenthal, a news photographer who accompanied the Marines to Iwo Jima to record the battle, prepared to capture the action. As the six soldiers struggled to push the iron flagpole up into the wind, Rosenthal swung his camera into position and snapped a single picture. The men watching from below and on nearby ships cheered and yelled as the flag rose in the sky.

Rosenthal's photograph turned out to be unforgettable. When people all across the United States saw the picture on the front page of their Sunday newspapers, they were awestruck. Tears came to the eyes of many. Americans everywhere were filled with gratitude at the sight of those brave young men raising their country's flag in the middle of a terrible battle.

The Marines finally won the battle for Iwo Jima thirty-six days after landing there. Thousands were wounded or killed, including three of the men who raised the flag with Ira.

When the three survivors returned home, they were treated like heroes. Ira was shocked to find thousands of people cheering for him. He didn't think he deserved all the attention. Ira told the crowds that the soldiers who died on Iwo Jima and in other battles were the real heroes.

Separated from his Marine buddies and surrounded by strangers, Ira's loneliness returned. Yet whenever people saw him, they wanted to celebrate. They bought Ira alcoholic drinks and praised the quiet Pima Indian for his heroic deed. The drinks helped Ira cope with his feelings of being alone.

Felix de Weldon, an artist serving in the United States Navy, was spellbound by Rosenthal's photograph. He thought the courage shown in the picture reflected America's will to win the war. De Weldon immediately went to work on a small statue, sculpting the bent knees and straining muscles of the six determined young men raising the flag. Ira stood at the back of the group, his helping hands raised high above his head, just as in the photograph.

Shortly after, de Weldon was asked to re-create his statue on a monumental scale. Everything about the sculpture would be gigantic—the boots, the helmets, the soldiers. The result was a colossal bronze statue, with thirty-two-foot-high figures raising a sixty-foot flagpole.

Ira found it hard to adjust to civilian life after the war. His loneliness deepened and turned to despair, and he drank more and more. Tragically, he died on January 24, 1955, just short of the tenth anniversary of raising the flag on Iwo Jima.

Ira Hamilton Hayes was buried on a grassy hillside in Arlington National Cemetery. America's quiet hero rests there among thousands of other servicemen and servicewomen who have fought for the United States, from the Revolutionary War to the present.

Nearby, in Washington D.C., is the majestic United States Marine Corps War Memorial. De Weldon's inspiring bronze statue stands there for everyone to see. Ira will forever be where he was happiest—with his Marine buddies. Together, this mountain of men raise the American flag in glory for all time.

*Private First Class
Ira Hamilton Hayes, 1945*

Had it not been for Joe Rosenthal's photograph, Ira Hayes would have been as unknown as thousands of other soldiers who fought for the United States in World War II. Naturally shy and withdrawn, Ira preferred to be left alone. As fate would have it, Rosenthal's photo turned this quiet man into a reluctant national hero.

Born in 1923, Ira Hayes grew up during the Great Depression of the 1930s. The United States experienced an extreme economic slump, and there was great unemployment and poverty across the country. On the Gila River Indian Reservation where Ira and his family lived, the hardships of daily living were particularly severe. Many families were near starvation. Indian parents, realizing their children would receive food and clothing at government-run schools, reluctantly sent their children away. These schools attempted to assimilate Native American children into the white American way of life.

Ira with his father, Joe E. Hayes

Ira Hayes attended several schools, the last one being Phoenix Indian School in Phoenix, Arizona. Phoenix Indian School opened in 1891. It housed students from many different tribes from third grade through high school. Initially the school operated with military-style discipline, with the goal of "civilizing" Indian children. Students wore uniforms; marched; and woke up, ate, studied, and went to bed on a strict schedule. Boys and girls were separated at all times. They were punished for speaking their native languages and observing traditional ceremonies. However, during the 1930s the general public began to demand equality for Native Americans. By the time Ira entered the

Students learning mathematics, Phoenix Indian School, 1940s

school in 1940, students no longer wore uniforms. Rules and schedules were regularly enforced, but strict punishment was reduced. Boys and girls attended the same classes, and were allowed to eat together and socialize. Most students developed a sense of comfort and felt their schooling provided them with many opportunities. But for some from isolated locations, such as Ira, the boarding school experience was foreign and frightening. Even so, the regimentation he endured prepared Ira for life in the military.

For many decades Indians had been subjected to severe discrimination and injustice at the hands of the United States government. Yet Native Americans were as patriotic as any citizens. When war threatened, young men looked beyond the injustices their people had suffered and did not hesitate to enlist in the military. Like so many other Americans, Native Americans were proud to serve and protect their country.

Toward the end of World War II, the island of Iwo Jima had great strategic importance because of the airfields located there. Under Japanese control, the island could be used as an early warning station and as a base for attacking American bombers on their flights to mainland Japan. Under United States control, the airfields could be used

Iwo Jima; Mount Suribachi at lower right

by American fighter planes that escorted the bombers and as emergency landing bases for airplanes damaged in bombing raids.

After a three-day air and naval bombardment, the U.S. Marines launched a massive attack on Iwo Jima on February 19, 1945. The Japanese soldiers defending the island fought from underground bunkers connected by a network of

Marines approaching Iwo Jima, February 19, 1945

tunnels. The Marines were aboveground, and the loose volcanic ash made it nearly impossible to dig foxholes. The Japanese soldiers vowed to kill as many Americans as possible and to die fighting. It took more than a month of fierce, bloody battle, but the United States finally won control of Iwo Jima on March 26. By then more than 21,000 Japanese were killed or committed suicide. Approximately 6,800 Americans died, and more than 17,000 were wounded.

Joe Rosenthal was an experienced combat photographer who accompanied the Marines as they battled their way across the Pacific Ocean toward Japan. He climbed to the

Flag raising atop Mount Suribachi, February 23, 1945; Ira Hayes at left

top of Mount Suribachi with the soldiers who were sent to put up the second flag. He took just one picture of the flag raising—and captured six determined figures in the midst of terrible conflict, united in one forward-moving, pyramid-

shaped mass. This inspiring image deeply touched the American people and helped reinforce their commitment to win the war. Joe Rosenthal was later awarded a Pulitzer Prize for his photograph, and it is believed to be the most reproduced photograph in history.

As a result of Rosenthal's photograph, Ira Hayes and the two other survivors of the flag raising, Rene Gagnon and John Bradley, were considered heroes. They were called back from the frontlines and asked to join a bond drive to

Ira Hayes (right), Rene Gagnon (left), and John Bradley with 7th War Loan Poster, 1945

raise money for the United States war effort. Overwhelmed by the public attention and the sudden loss of belonging and purpose, Ira drank to relieve his loneliness. Alcohol also helped him forget the horrors of war and numbed his feelings of despair over the terrible conditions endured by his family and others living on the Gila River Indian Reservation. Ira struggled to control his drinking for many years, but without treatment, alcoholism consumed him. He died on January 24, 1955, at the age of thirty-two.

The United States Marine Corps War Memorial in Washington, D.C., is the largest bronze statue in the world. Inspired by Joe Rosenthal's photograph, Felix de Weldon directed a team of artisans in the construction of the statue.

Felix de Weldon (left) with Rene Gagnon, Ira Hayes, and John Bradley in front of plaster cast of memorial statue

United States Marine Corps War Memorial, Washington, D.C.

First they shaped the six human figures in plaster. Then they formed a segmented mold of the entire mass, and molten bronze was cast into each mold segment. The bronze pieces were bolted and welded together. Completed in 1954, the gigantic statue stands seventy-eight feet high and weighs more than one hundred tons.

Ira Hayes was a humble, modest man who carried on the traditions of his people and fought honorably for his country during World War II. Although his life had a sad ending, he remains a symbol of courage, strength, and patriotism for all Americans. As President Harry Truman said upon Ira Hayes's return home from the Pacific, "You are an American hero."

S. D. Nelson

BIBLIOGRAPHY

Aarchuleta, Margaret L., Brenda J. Child, and K. Tsianina Lomawaima. *Away From Home: American Indian Boarding School Experiences.* Phoenix, AZ: Heard Museum, 2000.

Alexander, Joseph H. *Closing In: Marines in the Seizure of Iwo Jima.* Marines in World War II Commemorative Series. Washington, D.C.: U.S. Government Printing Office, 1994.

Bradley, James, and Ron Powers. *Flags of Our Fathers.* New York: Bantam Books, 2000.

Brinkley-Rogers, Paul. "A Fading Picture From Iwo Jima." *The Arizona Republic,* February 12, 1995.

Cash, Johnny, perf. "The Ballad of Ira Hayes," by Peter LaFarge. *Bitter Tears: Ballads of the American Indian.* Legacy Recordings, 1964. CD, 1994.

Hearn, Chester G. *An Illustrated History of the United States Marine Corps.* London: Salamander, 2002.

Hemingway, Albert. *Ira Hayes, Pima Marine.* Lanham, MD: University Press of America, 1988.

Jones, Charles A. "Into the Meat Grinder." *World War II,* March 2005, 46–53.

Lexton, Lauren, dir. *Heroes of Iwo Jima.* DVD and VHS. New York: A&E Home Video, 2001.

Marine Corps Legacy Museum. "Marine Corps Ribbon Display." http://www.mclm.com/gallery/ribbon.html

Marling, Karal Ann, and John Wetenhall. *Iwo Jima: Monuments, Memories, and the American Hero.* Cambridge, MA: Harvard University Press, 1991.

Parker, Dorothy R. *Phoenix Indian School: The Second Half-Century.* Tucson: University of Arizona Press, 1996.

Ropp, Thomas. "Reluctant Hero." *The Arizona Republic,* August 29, 1985.

Ross, Bill D. *Iwo Jima: Legacy of Valor.* New York: Vanguard Press, 1984.

Townsend, Kenneth William. *World War II and the American Indian.* Albuquerque: University of New Mexico Press, 2000.

Trennert, Robert A. *The Phoenix Indian School: Forced Assimilation, 1891–1935.* Norman: University of Oklahoma Press, 1988.

Wenz, Karen L. "Ira Hayes: His Story and a Detailed Annotated Bibliography." Master of Arts thesis, St. Cloud State University. St. Cloud, MN, 1998.